D0889978

WITHDRAWN
BLUE RIDGE LIBRARY
28 AVERY ROW
ROANOKE, VA 24012

0 1191 0333786 9

SKATEBOARDING TIPS AND TRICKS™

RIDING BOWLS AND POOLS

**PETER MICHALSKI
AND JUSTIN HOCKING**

rosen publishing's
rosen
central®

BLUE RIDGE LIBRARY
28 Avery Row
Roanoke, VA 24012

Published in 2017 by The Rosen Publishing Group, Inc.
29 East 21st Street, New York, NY 10010

Copyright © 2017 by The Rosen Publishing Group, Inc.

First Edition

All rights reserved. No part of this book may be reproduced in any form without permission in writing by the publisher, except by a reviewer.

Library of Congress Cataloging-in-Publication Data

Names: Michalski, Pete, author. | Hocking, Justin.
Title: Riding bowls and pools / Peter Michalski and Justin Hocking.
Description: First Edition. | New York : Rosen Central, 2017. | Series:
  (Skateboarding Tips and Tricks) | Includes bibliographical references,
  webography and index.
Identifiers: LCCN 2016008876| ISBN 9781477788684 (Library Bound) | ISBN
  9781477788660 (Paperback) | ISBN 9781477788677 (6-pack)
Subjects: LCSH: Skateboarding—Juvenile literature.
Classification: LCC GV859.8 .M53 2017 | DDC 796.22—dc23
LC record available at http://lccn.loc.gov/2016008876

Manufactured in China

CONTENTS

INTRODUCTION

Whether you are used to street skating, street courses, or ripping it on half-pipes, there is a whole world of skateboarding out there for you to experience. One of the most fun ways of skating is in empty pools and bowls.

Bowls are a kind of ramp with rounded curves, called transitions, that go all the way around. Picture an irregularly shaped cereal or salad bowl. Before bowls were built specifically for skaters to use, the same type of skating was done in empty and abandoned pools. In fact, this was really the first example of vert skating, and it developed, by most accounts, in California during the mid-1960s. People have been skating in bowls and empty pools for decades.

Perhaps you have already skated a bowl or a pool here and there. You may have one near you and want to get into some more advanced tricks. First, you need some basic ramps skills to start out with.

From bowl skating fundamentals and basics, this resource will help you move on to harder maneuvers—like grinds, airs, and hip transfers, among other tricks.

Whatever skill level you are, learning more about bowl and pool skating is fun, and it makes you a more well-rounded skater. So grab your board, drop in, and take advantage of the exciting world of riding bowls and pools.

Isabelle Caudle, a forty-three-year-old mother, drops into a bowl in Laguna Niguel, California. She belongs to Skateboarding Moms, an all-ages skate crew.

CHAPTER ONE

BOWLS AND POOLS: KNOW THE TERRAIN

It may seem incredible, but skateboarding has been around for more than seventy years, although it only became truly well known in the 1960s and 1970s. If you had a time machine, you could go back to when it first started to take off. Skating was probably invented by surfers in the late 1940s who looking for something to do when they were away from the beach.

As you step out of your time machine, you might see a group of kids rolling down the street barefoot, making slalom turns on planks of wood with roller skate wheels nailed to the bottom. They're moving pretty slowly, and with metal wheels, they take a slam, or fall, every time they hit even the smallest pebble.

Back then, skateboarding was mainly a form of transportation, and the only tricks were things like rolling handstands, high jumps, and hang tens, where the skater rides with both feet on the nose and all ten toes hanging off the front of the board. These skaters would have known nothing about ollies or similar tricks. Boards were flat back then, and the angled kicktail that you find on the back of almost all modern skateboards hadn't even been invented.

POOL SKATING: THE 1960S

Moving forward to the 1960s, you might witness something that changed the face of skateboarding forever. At some point, skateboarders discovered that empty backyard swimming pools were ideal skating venues, with their smoothly rounded transitions and blue tile. No one knows who the first person to skate in a pool was, but the first pool sessions can be traced as far back as 1963 to legendary skater Gary Swanson's backyard pool.

Pool riding took off in the late 1960s and 1970s, aided by the introduction of urethane wheels, a type of plastic wheel that allows skateboards to roll much faster and smoother than clay or metal wheels. Skaters in places like Venice Beach (also known as Dogtown) brought many of surfing's aggressive, flowing moves to pool skating. Instead of just doing handstands and other gymnastic tricks on flat sidewalks, these skaters understood that skating a pool was like riding a giant concrete

Pool pioneer and legend Mike Weed (1958–2014) is shown here in a 1977 photo taken in Toronto, Ontario.

wave. Legendary skaters like Tony Alva and Jay Adams were doing what seemed impossible a few years earlier: grinding and catching airs in backyard pools. These skaters helped change a freestyle-oriented, acrobatic fad into a more aggressive, surf-style pursuit.

POOLS AND BOWLS: HOW ARE THEY DIFFERENT?

Pools and bowls are basically the same thing. However, the term "pool" is usually used to describe actual backyard swimming pools that weren't originally built for skateboarding.

Backyard pools are fun, but they have several drawbacks, too. First of all, the chances of actually finding backyard pools to skate in are pretty slim. If you do find one, chances are it might be on private property. With extremely steep transitions, backyard pools are among the most difficult to skate.

Fortunately, you can now find concrete or wooden bowls at many skateparks nationwide. They're very similar to pools. In fact, some bowls, like the one at the

A young skater does a trick off the lip of a bowl at the famous Laguna Hills skatepark.

Donald Skatepark in Oregon, are exact replicas of swimming pools.

Most skatepark bowls have much more mellow transitions, making them ideal for learning basic skills. The tricks in this resource are mostly for wooden bowls and skatepark pools. This is where we recommend you start out.

ELEMENTS OF A BOWL

Before you start getting busy in a bowl, you should learn the different elements of the bowl environment. First of all, many bowls and pools are made out of concrete. Concrete is the material of choice for a lot of reasons: it never wears out, it allows skaters to ride fast, and it can be shaped into all sorts of cool curves and forms.

ROCK HARD: BEWARE CONCRETE

One drawback to concrete is how hard it is. Few things hurt worse than a hard slam on concrete. Although slamming in a bowl never feels good, no matter what surface you land on, wooden bowls tend to give, or flex, just a little when you slam, which makes it a little less painful. However, wooden bowls are hard to build. It's a huge challenge to make concave curves using wood. But there are plenty of them out there, and they're usually surfaced with materials such as masonite, birch plywood, or the weather-resistant Skatelite.

The transitions, also called trannys or walls, are the curving sections of the bowl or pool, the parts that look like the vertical face of a frozen wave. The corners are the horizontally curving sections that connect the transitions. These are what give the bowl its rounded, cereal bowl shape. Many bowls are shaped this way, but most modern bowls have more unique shapes with at least a few "flat" walls, or straight, sections, to break up the corners and allow for more complex and interesting lines.

Another common bowl feature is a hip, which is where two transitions meet at an angle and jut out like an actual hip. A pool with a single hip is often called a kidney pool because it resembles the shape of a kidney bean.

The flat bottom is the flat, ground-level section of the bowl that separates the transitions. Most bowls have at least 10 feet (3 meters) of flat bottom, making it easier to set up for your next trick because it gives you

A skater pulls off a crail slide—a tailside grab with the back hand on the heel side of the nose—along the pool wall extension.

time until you reach the opposite transition. But many backyard pools have little or no flat bottom, which means you have to be quick on your feet.

At the top of each transition is a round metal pipe known as the coping or the lip. The coping is a surface for doing grinds and stalls, and bouncing your wheels off the coping helps you pop up above the bowl on aerial tricks.

In many backyard pools, above a row of ornamental tiles, you will find the concrete coping. Sometimes known as pool coping, this is much rougher than metal coping and may have lots of cracks and seams. Because of its rough surface, you need more speed and power to grind concrete coping. For many skaters, that is an attraction, rather than a drawback, and they actively seek the loud "barking" sounds of metal trucks grinding on the concrete.

Atop each transition, you'll find a deck. This is where skaters stand before taking their next "plunge"—that is, dropping into the pool or bowl.

CHAPTER TWO

LEARNING THE FUNDAMENTALS

Now that you are familiar with pool skating's origins and the elements of bowls, you are probably impatient to get in there and show your stuff. Not so fast, however. Bowl and pool skating are fun, but they also require great care. Being unprepared and/or overconfident is dangerous.

The first step is to protect your body and your head so you can live to skate another day if you suffer any kind of spill or other accident. Always wear pads and a good helmet. No exceptions. And make sure to invest in gear made for skating because pads for other sports (like soccer pads) just will not cut it.

Companies like Rector, Protec, and Boneless all make top-of-the-line pads, the kind with a thick plastic cap over the kneecap. If you've ever seen people skate a half-pipe or bowl, then you know exactly what this cap is for: when you bail a trick, instead of flopping like a dead fish to the flat bottom, experienced skaters drop to their knees and slide gracefully down the transition on their knee pads. Before you start

Can you figure out why this picture is an example of what not to do when you hit a bowl or pool as a newbie? Neither the girl holding the board in the foreground nor her friend skating the lip have helmets on.

actually skating a bowl, it's a good idea to practice some knee slides without your skateboard.

THE KNEE SLIDE

1. Run a few feet up the transition.
2. As you near the top of the bowl, turn around and jump to your knees.
3. Slide down the transition on your plastic kneecaps with your feet dragging beneath you. Place some weight on

your feet but avoid sitting down too hard on your heels, which could lead to an ankle or foot injury.

4. As you slide, lean back a little. If you start to fall forward, instead of putting your hands out in front of you and risking an arm or wrist injury, fall onto your elbow pads and use them to slide, the same way you slide on your knee pads. It's sort of an awkward position, but you'll get used to it.

5. Try working your way higher up the ramp and doing longer slides. If you're practicing in a smaller wooden bowl, you can also try scooting into a knee slide from the deck. Once you actually start skating the bowl, it'll take a little practice to get in the habit of dropping to your knees when you take a fall. Learning to knee slide will definitely help keep you safe, but it's not a 100 percent guarantee against injury.

The truth is, if you're a skateboarder, you'll bang yourself up a little at some point. It comes with the territory, but the best way to protect yourself against serious injuries is to use your head and skate smart. It's good to push yourself and take risks, but the most important thing is to be smart and progress at your own pace. Attempting a trick that you're not ready for or trying to show off are two of the main reasons people get hurt in bowls or pools. Remember, skateboarding is not a competitive

A boarder stands ready to drop in. The pads she is wearing protect her knees from serious damage.

WATCH AND LEARN

Whenever you show up to a bowl or pool, especially one you've never skated before, there's another important way you need to use your head . . . and your eyes. If there are people already skating, sit down and just watch them for a while. Pay attention to how they skate, where they drop in, and what type of lines they take. That way, once you start skating, you'll have a better understanding of the bowl itself, and you can avoid getting in anyone's way. Along with watching what kind of lines other skaters take, it's important to pay attention to the order that skaters go in. It's OK to jump into a session, but make sure to wait your turn before you take your next run.

sport. You don't have to worry about trying to prove yourself to anyone. So skate smart because it's really all about just having fun with your friends.

CARVING

The thing that makes skating bowls fun is that, unlike in a half-pipe where you just go back and forth, you can do what's called carving. Carving allows you to move in circular patterns around the bowl, using the corners to gain momentum and speed. Once you learn how to do it, you'll find that the cool thing about carving is that it allows you to go fast, and if you want to, really fast. In fact, some people enjoy simply carving in a bowl without really doing many tricks at all.

Two riders carve in a pool, one hot on the other's tail. Until you build your skills, you should probably avoid riding too close to other skaters.

Before you learn to carve, you should definitely be comfortable with pumping, dropping in, and doing kickturns on a half-pipe. If you don't already have these skills wired, it's a good idea at this point to go back and read the book *Riding Half-Pipes* in the Skateboarding Tips and Tricks series.

When you skate a ramp, you maintain speed by using your legs to apply downward force on the skateboard as you move up and down each transition. This is called pumping. Many of the same pumping motions help you keep your speed in a bowl, too. But carving through a corner is just a little different than pumping in a half-pipe. Think of the corner itself as a half-pipe turned on its side. As you move through it, even though you're up on the wall, you have to pump, just like you would in a regular ramp.

Before you try carving, it's usually a good idea to grab a skate key or a wrench and loosen your trucks up a bit, especially if you normally ride with very tight trucks. To loosen your trucks, use your skate key or wrench to turn your large truck bolt counterclockwise a few spins. This makes it much easier to skate a bowl because it allows you to make sharper turns simply by leaning on your toes or heels. And before you try the next five steps, try doing a few basic kickturns in the bowl, just to warm up.

To do a kickturn, you press down on your tail with your back foot as you ride up the transition, then lift your front wheels off the ramp and turn 180 degrees back toward the other side of the bowl. Here's a step-by-step approach to carving backside:

TRICK:

1. Approach the corner in the backside fashion (which means you'll be turning in the direction toward your toes) with your knees bent slightly. Don't ride straight into the corner. Instead, approach it at a very wide, arching angle.
2. Your front foot should be directly above the mounting bolts for your front truck, while your back foot should rest in the spot where your tail starts to angle up. Since you're carving backside, press down slightly on the edge of your board with your toes and the balls of your feet, just like you would to turn backside in the street.
3. As you enter the corner, avoid the temptation to lift up your front wheels like you would for a kickturn. In a true carve, you keep all four wheels on surface of the ramp (also known as "four on the floor"). If you're having trouble, try loosening your trucks some more.

4. As you enter the corner, press down on the board, lean forward, and stay pretty low. The more downward pressure you apply with your feet and legs, the faster you'll move through the corner.
5. Don't try to come straight down from the corner. Instead, angle down off the face wall, pumping as you come down the transition.

Carving frontside (which means you turn in the direction toward your heels) through a corner involves pretty much the same motions as backside, with a few important differences:

1. Approach the wall frontside, with your knees bent and your legs bowed out slightly. When you're first learning to carve frontside, you really have to work to get your knees bent, so it's OK if you squat a little.
2. It's a little harder to see where you're going when you carve frontside, so make sure to look over your lead shoulder as you turn. That way, you can see exactly where you're going.
3. As you enter the corner, avoid the temptation to lean toward the coping. In order to really carve and gain speed, you have to lean back a little toward the bowl as you use all the power in your feet and legs to press down on the skateboard and pump through the corner.
4. Since you're turning frontside, you'll need to apply some pressure with your heels on the edge of the board, just like if you were turning in the street.
5. Come out of your carve at a slight angle and stand up straight as you hit the flat bottom so that you're ready for the next wall.

Like half-pipes, bowls are shaped to provide maximum air when someone is trying to do aerial maneuvers.

If you've never tried carving before, it'll take some time and practice to get it down. You can pick up the basics in a day or two, but sometimes it takes a while before you really feel comfortable carving in a bowl. Be patient and persistent because you really need to have carving mastered before you move on to more advanced bowl tricks.

It is good to set small goals for yourself as you learn new tricks and progress from the basics to more challenging ones. One thing you can try is seeing how many corners you can carve in a single run. Work your way up higher toward the lip of the bowl. When you have started to get the hang of it, try coming out of a backside carve in one corner into a frontside carve in another corner, a line also known as a figure eight.

CHAPTER THREE

THE BASICS OF THE BOWL

As with anything—any sport or even any kind of pursuit—skating bowls is a progressive activity. You start somewhere and move forward. Like building a house begins with laying the foundation, getting to be a great bowl skater begins with the fundamentals. Among the most important is learning how to carve. Once you get that down, you are ready to move on to other tricks. Be patient, work hard, and you will get it.

The tricks in this resource are divided into three categories: basic, intermediate, and advanced. Naturally, basic tricks are the easiest to learn, and, like the rough framework built on top of a foundation, you need to start out with these before you add anything else. It is also recommended you learn most of the following tricks in a regular half-pipe before you attempt them in a bowl.

Pacing yourself and learning tricks in a particular order will help you build skill levels slowly. Jump the gun, and you risk taking on too much at once and getting discouraged, and even hurting yourself in the process.

CATCH A CARVE TRAIN

Once you and some friends master the fine art of carving, you're ready to catch a carve train. Trains are best with about three people—any more and it'll be more like a crash-up derby than a train.

So here's how it goes: the first person drops in and starts to carve through the bowl, followed by the second person, who follows the first person's lines. And then the third person does the same until you have a little skate train going. It's fun to see how long you can keep everyone together.

Trains are also good because when following a friend it forces you to try new lines. Make sure to watch out for each other, and always let the fastest skater go first so he or she doesn't run over slower buddies.

BACKSIDE GRINDS

Grinds are some of the most common and fun bowl tricks. A grind is a trick where your trucks make contact with and slide, or grind, along the coping.

There are all kinds of different grinds you can do, but first you need to get the basic grind down. If you can already do these on a regular half-pipe, they'll come pretty naturally in a bowl. And remember how we told you to keep four on the floor when carving? When learning basic carves in a bowl, it's OK to lift your front trucks and wheels off the surface, just like you would for a grind in a half-pipe.

This skater is executing a backside grind along the bowl wall lip.

1. Approach the corner with enough speed to reach the lip of the bowl.

2. As you begin your carve, raise your back heel just a bit and use your back toes to put a little extra pressure on the edge of your tail, which will also lift your front trucks and wheels over the coping. This makes it easier for your back wheel to roll over the coping so that your back truck can contact the lip.

3. As your back truck hits the coping, shift some of your weight to your back foot. Make sure you lean forward as you grind, staying low and keeping most of your body weight in toward the bowl.

4. As you complete your grind, again put some pressure on the edge of your tail. This will help to get your back truck and wheel off the coping smoothly.

5. Keep your knees bent and ride down the wall.

BASIC FRONTSIDE GRINDS

Once you get the basic backside grind down, it's time to learn the frontside grind. Although they're both basic grinds and they involve some similar motions, they feel completely different when you do them.

1. Carve into the corner with plenty of speed.
2. Use your toe and the ball of your foot to press down slightly on your tail.

A skater at Los Angeles's Venice Skatepark executes a frontside grind, one of the most enjoyable basic fundamentals of bowl and pool skating.

3. Lift up your front trucks and wheels, and let your back truck grind on the coping. Shift most of your weight to your back foot and keep your knees bent as you grind.
4. As you complete your grind, begin to turn your hips and shoulder back into the bowl.
5. Look over your lead shoulder and pump the transition as you ride back in.

CARVE GRINDS

Once you get the hang of simple grinds (some people call them scratcher grinds because you're basically just scratching the coping), you can try a slightly more advanced trick called the carve grind.

Carve grinds involve a motion similar to basic grinds, except that instead of lifting up your front trucks, you allow them to grind along with your back trucks. Carve grinds allow you to get more speed than a basic grind, and they'll also help you learn more advanced grinds like the 50-50. If you have basic carves down, they're really pretty simple:

1. Carve into the corner at a wider angle and with a little more speed than you would for a basic grind.
2. As you approach the lip, apply some pressure on the edge of your board with your toes and the balls of your feet. This will allow both your front and back trucks to contact the coping and grind.
3. As you grind, lean forward and keep your whole body in toward the bowl.
4. As your grind begins to end, again apply a little pressure with your toes and the balls of your foot. This will help get

your wheels and trucks off the coping so you can ride smoothly back into the bowl.

5. Once both your trucks are off the coping, carve back down the wall and ride into the flat bottom.

AXLE STALLS

Axle stalls are another important foundation trick that will eventually help you learn 50-50s in a bowl. They're also a good setup trick, which means they're the kind of basic trick that allows you to rest just for a second and prepare for harder tricks. To do an axle stall, you set both trucks square on the coping and stall for a moment. Here's how they're done:

1. Unlike a grind, for an axle stall you want to avoid carving and instead make more of a straight-line approach to the lip. You also need some extra speed to get all the way on top of the deck, but not so much that you overshoot the coping.

A skater moves into position to perform a stall at the lip of a bowl.

2. As you reach the top of the bowl, press down on your tail and lift up your front trucks so that they don't hit the coping.
3. Set your back truck on the coping first, putting some extra weight on your back heel so you can get your board and body all the way up on the deck.
4. Once your back truck is resting on the coping, use it as your pivot point, bringing your shoulders and hips around so they're parallel with the coping below you. Set your front trucks down, keeping the weight on your heels and your body leaning in toward the ramp.
5. After you stall for a second, press down on your tail with the toes of your back foot. Rotate your hips and shoulders, lean forward, and turn off the coping.
6. Ride back into the bowl.

BACKSIDE ROCK-AND-ROLLS

The rock-and-roll is a classic beginner bowl trick. Like the axle stall, the rock-and-roll is a good setup trick, too.

1. Without carving, ride straight up the transition with enough speed to reach the lip.
2. As you approach the lip, press down on the tail with your back foot and use your front foot to lift your front trucks and wheels over the coping. As you do this, begin to rotate your torso and shoulder backside, so that they're parallel with the coping.
3. Set the center of your board down on the coping by straightening out your front leg and using your foot to press your front truck and wheels down on the deck. At the

same time, bend your back knee. These two motions combined will make your back wheels come off the ramp in a rocking (or teetering) motion.

4. While your board stalls briefly on the coping and the deck, keep leaning your body back into the transition and continue rotating your upper body backside. This will make it easier to reenter the bowl.

5. As you begin to reenter press down on your tail, shifting weight off your front foot. This will allow you to lift your trucks and wheels back over the coping without getting caught up as you quickly turn back into the tranny. Continue rotating your body so that your shoulders and hips come all the way around and face the opposite side of the bowl.

6. Set your front trucks back down on the ramp, keeping your knees bent as you roll down the wall.

A good trick is not complete until you have safely rolled back down the transition from the lip of the bowl.

CHAPTER FOUR

BOWL TRICKS: FROM INTERMEDIATE TO ADVANCED

O nce you have all the beginner tricks down, it is time to step things up. If you are comfortable with carving, you are likely skating faster in the bowl. Speed will be key for the next round of tricks you will want to master.

One trick that definitely takes a little more speed is the 50-50 grind. The 50-50 is an essential bowl trick, and it helps you get speed for advanced tricks like airs and inverts. A 50-50 involves almost the same motions as an axle stall, except you actually grind across the coping instead of just stalling. Once you get 50-50s wired, try grinding though the entire corner.

50-50 GRINDS IN A CORNER

1. Make a wide carve into the corner, just like you would for a carve grind, but with a little more speed.
2. Instead of grinding your front truck like you would for a carve grind, lift your front truck up before you hit the coping (similar to an axle stall) and begin grinding on your back truck.

3. Once your back truck is locked in, set down your front truck.

4. As you grind on both trucks, put pressure on both your heels so that you stay up on the deck. But, at the same time, keep your body weight and torso in toward the bowl so that you don't roll out on the deck and you're ready to drop back in the bowl.

5. If your trucks are locked into the coping they'll naturally guide you through the bowl's curved shape. But you can use your toes and the balls of your feet to make slight corrections.

6. As you complete your grind, press down on your tail with the ball of your back foot while turning your hips and shoulders back into the bowl.

7. Keep your knees bent slightly, and as you drop back in head toward the opposite wall.

FRONTSIDE 5-0 IN A CORNER

The 5-0 is also sometimes called a stand-up grind because unlike the basic frontside grind, you actually stand all the way up on the coping as you grind. If you have trouble standing up on your grinds in a bowl with concrete coping, you might have to do a small, floating hop to get on the coping. Also, some people consider it cheating, but it sometimes helps to drag your back heel on the coping while you learn this trick.

1. Instead of riding straight into the corner, make a wide frontside carve up toward the lip.

As you begin to build your skills, you will probably find youself riding higher and farther away from the lip of the bowl itself in many of the tricks you perform.

2. As you reach the top of the bowl, begin to lift your front truck up so it doesn't hit the coping. Your weight should be on the balls of your feet and your toes.
3. As your back truck begins to grind, straighten out your back leg, putting most of your weight on your back foot. This makes it easier to grind on your back truck only.
4. Stand up all the way on the coping as you grind, leaning just slightly back toward the transition.
5. As your grind ends, put some pressure on your tail and start guiding your board back into the ramp.
6. Use your front foot to press down on the board so that your front truck and wheels touch back down on the bowl surface.
7. Bend your knees slightly as you roll back in.

BACKSIDE LAYBACK GRIND TO TAIL

The layback grind, like the rock-and-roll, is another classic, old school trick. To do this trick, you need to be able to do backside 50-50s.

1. Carve into the corner, the same way you would for a backside 50-50.
2. As you reach the lip, crouch down with your knees and start reaching toward the nose of your board with your lead hand. Press down slightly on your tail so that your front truck and wheels don't hit the coping.
3. As your back truck begins to grind, grab the nose with your lead hand and plant your back hand on the coping behind you.

4. Stay crouched as you grind and straighten out your back arm, using it to push yourself along the coping.
5. As you finish your grind, use your lead hand to turn the board 90 degrees, locking your tail on the coping in the drop-in position. For a cool variation, keep pushing with your arm so that you actually slide on your tail.
6. Push off the coping with your back hand to help you stand up and roll back into the bowl.

ADVANCED BOWL TRICKS

Now that you have some intermediate tricks under your belt, you're ready for the most difficult bowl tricks.

FRONTSIDE SMITH GRINDS

Smiths are some of the trickiest grinds, and you should definitely have frontside 5-0s on lockdown before you try them. A smith is a grind where your back truck is on the coping and your front truck is below the coping, so that you're actually sliding on the bottom of your board at the same time you grind.

1. Carve frontside into the bowl, the same way you would for a frontside 5-0.
2. Press down on your tail to lift up your front trucks and wheels as you approach the coping.
3. Lean back and bend your back knee as you begin to grind with your back truck. Once you're all the way on the coping, straighten out your front leg, point your toes, and push your nose down below the coping. The board should be in such a position so that the bottom of your board near your front toe actually slides.

This 1985 image from a competition at Del Mar Skate Ranch in California shows skate veteran Allen Losi doing a frontside smith grind.

4. As you grind, keep your weight on your back truck, which will keep you locked in to the smith position
5. Once you complete your grind, press down on your tail with your heel to get your back truck off the coping. Begin to turn your shoulders and hips back into the ramp.
6. Bend your knees slightly as you roll back into the bowl and prepare for your next trick.

FRONTSIDE AIRS OVER A HIP

In order to do airs over a hip, it helps to be comfortable doing regular frontside airs in a half-pipe.

However, some people find that hip airs are actually easier than regular airs. And different people have different ways of doing hip airs. Some skaters snap their tail and pop an ollie before grabbing the board. Others simply bounce (or, as most people call it, bonk) their wheels on the coping and then let their momentum boost them into the air, without hitting their tail. We recommend you try the non-ollie method first, and then if you want more height, you can learn to pop into the trick.

A skater does a frontside air over the hip. Skate legend Tony Alva is often credited with inventing the frontside air.

1. Approach the hip at a slight angle. Your weight should be on the balls of your feet and your toes.
2. Press down on your tail a bit as you reach the coping in order to lift your front trucks over and bonk your wheels off the coping.
3. As you launch in the air, lean back and suck your knees up toward your body, lifting your board high enough for

you to grab. Reach down with your back hand and let the board float up into your grip. Once you grab, pull up on the board and slightly tuck your body.

4. Getting in the air is pretty easy. It's landing that's tricky. So here's the secret: when you're up in the air, look down and spot the exact point on the wall where you'll land.

5. Let go of the board before you set it down and keep your knees bent as you ride smoothly down the other side of the hip.

LINKING YOUR TRICKS

One of the best things about skating a bowl is that, as long as you keep carving and pumping, you can keep going and going without ever taking your back foot off to push like you would in the street. And the best bowl skaters don't just drop in, do one trick, and then jump back on the deck. Instead, they take long, flowing runs, working every part of the bowl and using figure-eight carves to shift from frontside to backside tricks.

For instance, if you're skating a bowl with a shallow end connected to a deep end, you might try dropping into a carve grind in the deep end. Then pump back up to the shallow for a frontside 5-0, and then back into the deep end for a backside layback grind or a frontside air. This is just an idea, of course. The most fun thing about skating is being creative and coming up with your own original combinations and lines.

A skater reaches for the sky doing a backside air. Some skaters insist that a true backside air needs to be at least three feet off the lip.

BACKSIDE AIRS

To do a backside air, you launch out of the bowl backside and grab the board with your lead hand. It's a pretty tough one to pull off in a bowl. This is one trick that's actually easier to learn in a steeper, larger bowl because the vert actually launches you up in the air.

1. Approach the lip backside with tons of speed.
2. Press down on your tail as you approach the coping. Let your back wheels bonk off the coping and lean into the bowl as you begin to reach down toward the board with your lead hand.
3. Grab the board anywhere from your nose to behind your front foot, whatever feels best for you.
4. Keep your body tucked and leaning forward as you reach the peak of your air. Before you start to come down, spot the point on the transition where you'll land.
5. Let go of the board as you start to come down. Be careful not to get your back wheels caught on the coping as you land.
6. Set the board down and roll down the wall.

GLOSSARY

backside Any trick in which you turn in the direction of your toes.

bail Another name for falling off your skateboard. A hard fall is usually called a slam.

bowl ramp A ramp with concave transitions all the way around, like a giant mixing bowl.

carving A method of riding through a bowl or pool in a way that increases your speed.

frontside Any trick in which you turn in the direction of your heels.

half-pipe A ramp with two opposing walls so that it dips down in the middle and back up on either side.

line Linking together a whole series of different tricks, rather than just doing a single trick, while utilizing many of the bowl's features.

lockdown A term used to describe a trick that a skater can land almost every time.

rip To skate with a lot of skill, style, speed, and consistency.

session A meeting where two or more skaters get together and skate.

skate key A small tool used for tightening or loosening the trucks of a skateboard.

stall A trick that involves balancing your board on something for a few seconds without moving forward and then pulling off the object.

street skating Skating without using any ramps or anything but found obstacles.

tail The tail is the rear part of that skateboard that angles upward.

truck The metal device that holds the wheels of a skateboard to the deck and that makes it possible to turn.

wired The same as lockdown, it is a term used to describe a trick that is mastered.

Go Skateboarding Foundation
22431 Antonio Parkway
Rancho Santa Margarita, CA 92688
(949) 455-1112
Website: http://goskateboardingfoundation.org
The Go Skateboarding Foundation provides education, career
    programming, and scholarships, and helps fund skateparks.

International Skateboarding Federation (ISF)
P.O. Box 57
Woodward, PA 16882
(814) 883-5635
Website: http://www.internationalskateboardingfederation.com
The International Skateboarding Federation (ISF) is formally orga-
    nized and incorporated to provide direction and governance
    for the sport of skateboarding worldwide.

Skatepark Association of the United States of America (SPAUSA)
2210 Lincoln Boulevard
Venice, CA 90291
Website: http://www.spausa.org
The Skatepark Association of the United States of America
    (SPAUSA) is a nonprofit organization that assists communities
    obtain the resources to build their own skateparks.

Skaters for Public Skateparks
820 North River Street, Loft 206
Portland, OR 97227
Website: http://www.skatepark.org
Skaters for Public Skateparks is a nonprofit advocacy group that
   provides information to those hoping to finance, build, and/or
   improve their local skateparks and other skating venues.

WEBSITES

Because of the changing nature of Internet links, Rosen
Publishing has developed an online list of websites related to the
subject of this book. This site is updated regularly. Please use this
link to access this list:

http://www.rosenlinks.com/STT/bowl

Brooke, Michael. *The Concrete Wave: The History of Skateboarding.* Toronto, ON: Warwick Publishing, 1999.

Davis, Gary, and Craig Steycyk. *Dysfunctional.* Corte Madera, CA: Gingko Press, 1999.

Doeden, Matt. *Skateparks: Grab Your Skateboard.* Mankato, MN: Capstone Press, 2002.

Goodfellow, Evan, and Doug Werner. *Street Skateboarding: Endless Grinds and Slides: An Instructional Look at Curb Tricks.* Chula Vista, CA: Tracks Publishing, 2005.

Hawk, Tony. *Hawk: Occupation: Skateboarder.* New York, NY: Reagan Books, 2000.

Irvine, Alex, and Paul Parker. *So You Think You're a Skateboarder?: 50 Tales from the Street and the Skatepark.* New York, NY: CICO Books, 2014.

Lombard, Kara-Jane, ed. *Skateboarding: Subcultures, Sites, and Shifts* (Routledge Research in Sport, Culture, and Society). New York, NY: Routledge, 2015.

Marcus, Ben. *The Skateboard: The Good, the Rad, and the Gnarly.* Minneapolis, MN: MVP Books/Lerner Publishing, 2011.

Michalski, Peter, and Justin Hocking. *Riding Half-Pipes* (Skateboarding Tips and Tricks). New York, NY: Rosen Publishing, 2017.

Michalski, Peter, and Justin Hocking. *Riding Street Courses* (Skateboarding Tips and Tricks). New York, NY: Rosen Publishing, 2017.

Nixon, James. *Skateboarding Champion* (How to Be a Champion). New York, NY: Franklin Watts/Scholastic, 2015.

Rosenberg, Aaron. *Advanced Skateboarding*. New York, NY: Rosen Publishing, 2016.

Snyder, Craig B. *A Secret History of the Ollie, Volume 1: The 1970s.* Cambridge, MA: Black Salt Press, 2015.

Thatcher, Kevin. *Thrasher Presents How to Build Skateboard Ramps: Halfpipes, Boxes, Bowls and More.* San Francisco, CA: High Speed Productions, 2001.

Thrasher Magazine. *Thrasher: Insane Terrain*. New York, NY: Universe Publishing, 2001.

BIBLIOGRAPHY

Badillo, Beal, and Dan Werner. *Skateboarding: Book of Tricks* (Start-Up Sports) Chula Vista, CA: Tracks Publishing, 2003.

Beal, Becky. *Skateboarding: The Ultimate Guide*. Santa Barbara, CA: ABC-CLIO, 2013.

Brooke, Michael. *The Concrete Wave.* Toronto, ON: Warwick Publishing, Inc. 1999.

Mullen, Rodney. *The Mutt: How to Skateboard and Not Kill Yourself.* New York, NY: IT Books/HarperCollins, 2004.

Pointx.com. "Contact Us" (http://www.pointx.com. contact_us.asp).

Savage, Jeff. *Street Skating: Grinds and Grabs*. Mankato, MN: Capstone Press, 2005.

Skateboard.com. "Camps" (http://www.skateboard.com/frontside/GetLocal/camps/default.asp).

Skateboardpark.com. "Iowa City Skatepark" (http://www.skateboardpark.com/skateboardpark/viewpark.asp?ID=471).

Skateboardparks.com. "Verified Skateboard Parks" (http://www.skateboardparks.com/verified.html).

Skatecity.com. "Where to Skate: Skateparks." Retrieved February 22, 2004 (http://www.skatecity.com/nyc/where/parks.html#pier26).

Thatcher, Kevin. *Thrasher Presents How to Build Skateboard Halfpipes: Halfpipes, Boxes, Bowls and More*. San Francisco, CA: High Speed Productions, 2001.

Vansskatecamp.com. "Skate—Summer 2004" (http://www.vansskatecamp.com/index.htm).

Weyland, Jocko. *The Answer Is Never*. New York, NY: Grove Press, 2002.

Wixon, Ben. *Skateboarding: Instruction, Programming and Park Design*. Champaign, IL: Human Kinetics, 2009.

INDEX

ABOUT THE AUTHORS

Peter Michalski is a young-adult, nonfiction author who has penned many instructional titles for teens, covering sports, careers, and health issues.

Justin Hocking lives and skateboards in New York City. He is also an editor of the book *Life and Limb: Skateboarders Write from the Deep End*, published in 2004 by Soft Skull Press.

PHOTO CREDITS

Cover (skateboarder) Fuse/Thinkstock; cover (background), pp. 1, 6, 12, 20, 28 Jon Bilous/Shutterstock.com;p. 3 Dizzo/Vetta/ Getty Images; pp. 4-5 mgs/Moment Open/Getty Images; p. 5 (inset) Allen J. Schaben/ Los Angeles Times/Getty Images; p. 7 Dick Loek/Toronto Star/Getty Images; p. 8 Don Kelsen/Los Angeles Times; p. 10 Connor Walberg/The Image Bank/Getty Images; p. 13 Colin Anderson/Blend Images/Getty Images; p. 14 © Theo Fitzhugh/Alamy Stock Photo; p. 16 Connor Walberg/ Photonica/Getty Images; p. 19 ullstein bild/Getty Images; p. 22 © iStockphoto.com/carrollphoto; p. 23 cdrin/Shutterstock.com; p. 25 Ryan McVay/Photodisc/Thinkstock; p. 27 Sean Justice/ The Image Bank/Getty Images; p. 30 Daniel Brunner/E+/Getty Images; p. 33 Doug Pensinger/Getty Images; p. 34 Christian Carroll/iStock/Thinkstock; p. 36 Fairfax Media/Getty Images; back cover, interior pages (bricks) Ensuper/Shutterstock.com; interior pages banner textures Naburalna/Shutterstock.com

Designer: Michael Moy; Editor: Philip Wolny;
Photo Researcher: Karen Huang and Philip Wolny

BLUE RIDGE LIBRARY
28 AVERY ROW
ROANOKE, VA 24012